Scripture Study Book

New Testament

Reverend Steven M. Lanza

Harcourt Religion Publishers

www.harcourtreligion.com

Nihil Obstat
Reverend Steven Olds, S.T.D.
Censor Deputatus

Imprimatur
✠ Most Reverend Thomas G. Wenski, Bishop of Orlando
February 1, 2005

Printed in the United States of America

ISBN
0159016681

Contents

A Tool for Understanding

This book is meant as a tool to help you explore, discern, and study certain aspects of God's revelation found within Sacred Scripture. The book specifically presents selected passages found in the New Testament. The Church's teaching and its living Tradition shed light on the meaning and importance of these particular passages. Through study and reflection, you can grow in faith and understanding of the truth of Christ's message.

A Mystery Shared

God is a mystery. We only know something about God because he has chosen to tell and show us about himself. The pattern of this revelation unfolds throughout human history. We can explore, discern, and study this pattern of revelation in the Bible. The texts that make up the Bible were recorded under the inspiration of the Holy Spirit. For this reason we describe these texts as Sacred Scripture.

Recorded and Lived

The God who reveals himself—the God described in Sacred Scripture—is not indifferent. He cares for us so much that he takes the initiative to offer us salvation in his Son, Jesus Christ. He wants us to be in his friendship, to have the grace, light, and peace of his kingdom.

The Hebrew Scriptures of the Old Testament point the way to Christ. They detail the centuries-long preparation of a just and loving God who provides for his people. The Christian scriptures of the New Testament communicate the fullness of that revelation. The God who spoke to humanity in ages past continues to speak to us today through the Church. The same Holy Spirit who inspired the human authors of Sacred Scripture continues to inspire the living tradition of the Church today. Through the Church the Good News of Christ is proclaimed to the whole world.

For you, middle age is a long way off! Imagine, however, for a moment where you will be in middle age. Undoubtedly, no matter what career you choose or what state or country you call home, you will have a number of close friends whom you have known for a long period of time. Some of these friends may date back to your grade school days. You may no longer live in close proximity, but, perhaps, you are still talking on the phone from time to time or corresponding via email.

When two people have been friends for a very long time, they enjoy a shared history, part of which is a result of the conversations they have had. Those conversations—even when the small details are lost—have helped to shape the relationship. Those conversations have also helped to shape both individuals into the persons they are.

Think of your friendships. The longer your have been friends with someone, the deeper the impact of all the conversations you have had over the years.

Your Conversation with Jesus

Why is this conversation important? When you first heard of Jesus through your family and others, a friendship was established. That friendship has always been two-sided: Jesus speaks to you, and you speak to Jesus.

A Way to Deepen Your Friendship

By using this book, you can deepen your friendship with Jesus. Going through the different Scripture exercises is like having a conversation with a friend you have known for many years. Actually, you have been and will continue to have a conversation with Jesus. This book brings that conversation into focus. It invites you to become more aware of the significance of your faith conversation with Jesus and the Church.

Actually, because you are a member of a faith community, the Church, it has been many-sided. Prayer, worship, Scripture, and Church teaching have shaped the conversation you have had with Jesus, and thus helped to shape whom you are today. Without this conversation in faith, you would be a different person.

This book furthers the lifelong conversation you have with Christ and brings selected portions of Sacred Scripture to bear on that conversation.
• Each chapter identifies two different selections from the New Testament.
• You will follow the same three-step process to explore each scriptural selection.
• In each of the three steps, you'll find questions to assist you in the faith conversation you are having.
• You'll have the chance to write your thoughts, reflect silently, and discuss in groups.
• In the first two parts you might find an FYI—an interesting fact or an explanation of cultural terms, historical meaning or use of words, or geographical and social information to help you interpret the passage in the original context in which it was written.
• In the third part you might find an FYI about Church practice that helps you apply the main message of the passage to your life.

A Quick Read

• This step directs you to consider Who, What, Where, When, Who with, and What with
• These questions give you a reason to read, help you focus, and make sure you've gotten the first level meaning.
• You might also find questions that lead you to consider when you have been in similar situations as the people in the passage, the audience originally intended, or the biblical writer himself.

1 Reading the Word of God 10 minutes

First, you must find the scriptural selection in your Bible and read it. You actually have to go to the Bible to find them. This emphasizes that the primary book and focus of this Scripture Study Book is Scripture itself. This book is merely the tool to help you access the revelation found in Sacred Scripture.

Like any piece of literature, the selection from Sacred Scripture has a literary form. It contains a particular subject matter that arises out of a specific context. It might be from a letter of Saint Paul addressed to an ancient Christian community, one of Jesus' parables, or a narrative from one of the Gospels.

In this first step, the questions direct you to identify some of the basic aspects of the passage so that you can understand the Scripture on a primary level. These questions give a specific purpose for reading the Scripture, so you'll want to keep them in mind as you read.

2 Going Deeper into the Word of God 30 minutes

This next step takes you beyond a surface reading of the text of Sacred Scripture. Why is this important?

Staying on the surface level of Sacred Scripture limits our understanding. For example, the Parable of the lost sheep is not just a nice story told by Jesus about wayward sheep and a caring shepherd. This parable is about humanity who turns away from God, yet God loves us so much that he comes after us to find us and save us.

Another example is St. Paul's First Letter to the Corinthians. This letter is not merely addressed to an ancient Greek Christian community torn apart by dissension and disagreement. It can be understood to address us today as we grapple with similar issues of unity and holiness of life.

So, the book presents the deeper significance of these selections from Sacred Scripture in relation to Church teaching. Over the centuries many wise persons of faith have explored these same Scriptures. From these explorations, a certain perspective has developed that helps us to understand Scripture. The conversation we have with Christ is never done in isolation.

None of us invent our own faith. Your relationship with God is a gift that you receive from the Church. If it were your faith alone, then you might be tempted to cut out those portions of it that you do not like or that you find distasteful. If faith were a matter of your own invention, you could ignore or reinterpret certain aspects of the Good News. For example, you may fear death. So, when you read about the cross of Jesus, you may gloss over the Gospel accounts that talk about how Jesus actually suffered and died. You may reinterpret this aspect to "fit" with your own fears: Jesus only seemed to suffer and die. Or you may disregard the very real call in the Gospel that to be a disciple of Jesus, you are asked to take up your own cross.

Both the comments and the questions in this second step are meant to deepen your understanding of the scriptural selections.

A More In-Depth Consideration

• The questions in this part move into the meaning of the passage itself, asking how, what for, why, what next, how else.
• Sometimes you'll find questions that challenge you to identify with the meaning, consider implications or challenges that come from the Scripture reading, or make connections to other Church teachings or practices.

3 Applying the Word of God to our Lives

15 - 20 minutes

The whole point of faith reaches beyond us as individuals. Faith is meant to change us so that we can change the world.

The Letter of James in the New Testament challenges us: show me your faith and I will show you my works! A person can claim again and again to have faith. However, the proof of faith is in the works that are being done. To say this in another way: talk is cheap; actions speak louder than words or claims to faith.

This third step takes the word of God in Scripture and applies it to the actual circumstances of our lives. In this way, our faith will be made more apparent in what we say and do.

God has revealed himself to us. God expects a response. As Scripture reminds us, "Be doers of the word and not hearers only..." (James 1:22).

A New Way to Look at Life

• The questions in this part prompt reflection on your life and the ways in which the main scriptural themes can influence it.
• You may be asked to evaluate your choices, actions, experiences, and life situations in light of the theological themes discussed in the prior two steps.

Called into Relationship

Have you ever made a new friend because you were introduced to them by a current friend? Have you ever been brought into a whole circle of friends because of your friendship with one friend? Jesus, the Son of God, invites us into relationship with his Father and the Holy Spirit. Because of this relationship, we are included in a vast circle of friendship, the Church.

Reading the Word of God

Hebrews
8:7–13 and 9:11–15

These passages from the Letter to the Hebrews refer to the two biblical ways of relating to God. The "he" in Hebrews 8:8 and 8:13 refers to God. Think about the questions below before reading the passages directly from the Bible. After reading the passages, record your answers.

What are the two ways of relating to God and which is preferred?

The second passage from Hebrews describes many things. *What do you think is its main subject?*

Many laws regulate the old covenant, far more than simply the Ten Commandments.

- You can find most of the laws of the old covenant in the first five books of the Old Testament.

- Approximately 600 laws exist, corresponding, some say, to the bones in the human body. Just as our bones give our muscles a structure, the rules for worshiping and living as God's people were meant to provide a structure for Israel's faith.

OUR MEDIATOR

A mediator resolves a conflict between two parties. When we sin, we separate ourselves from God. In effect, when we sin, we are in conflict with God. Jesus, mediator between humanity and heaven, brings us back into a holy relationship with God the Father.

Jesus is not only a mediator, but also our friend. *Is there something specific that he can mediate between you and God the Father?*

Going Deeper into the Word of God

 As a group, reread Hebrews 9:11 — 14. Discuss how the author parallels practices of the old covenant with Jesus' sacrifice.

 *Discuss in what ways you welcome Christ into your life?*

Nothing from the Temple remains today, except the West Wall, commonly referred to as the "wailing wall." In Jesus' day the Temple was the center of ritual worship in Israel. For example, every male Jew was required to travel there yearly and offer a sacrifice to God. A small dove or goat would be sacrificed on the altar as prayers were made.

ACCESS TO GOD

Jesus is not just a wise and holy prophet. He is the Son of God. God himself takes the initiative and reaches out to us—even though we are sinners. God loves us so much that he sacrifices himself for our sakes. Hebrews relies on a powerful image to convey this point. It refers to the sanctuary Christ enters with his own blood (Hebrews 9:12). This image alludes to the Temple worship. Specifically it refers to the Inner Room of the great Temple in Jerusalem.

ONCE AND FOR ALL

Three of the four Gospel accounts report that at the moment Jesus died on the cross, the veil of the sanctuary was torn apart (Matthew 27:51, Mark 15:38 and Luke 23:46). Why? By Jesus' loving sacrifice on our behalf, the Holy of Holies has been opened so that all might have access to God. This sacrifice, says Hebrews, is effective once for all (Hebrews 9:12). No longer will we have to offer doves, goats, or anything else as a sacrifice. No longer will we need to rely on a Temple high priest to intercede for us. God's own sacrifice is enough.

Describe a time you put the needs of someone else before your own. *Why did you do so?*

After you've divided into two groups, have each group read aloud alternating verses from Hebrews 8:8–12, starting with the word "Behold. . ." Then, spend some quiet time considering the reflection below.

WE NEED A SAVIOR

Because we are human, we are probably going to break rules at some point. Fortunately, a faithful relationship with God is not determined only by following rules and regulations.

We need a savior who offers us mercy and forgiveness when we fail. Just as important, if not more, we also need a savior who shows us, by his own life and work in the world, how to live. It is like having a really good friend whom we admire for heroism or goodness, whom we are compelled to emulate. We can keep learning from our savior, growing in goodness, exceeding our own expectations, and surprising ourselves. We grow, exceed expectations, and surprise ourselves because we are motivated by the friendship we have with our savior.

If you had the privilege of introducing Jesus to your other friends, what would you say about him?

How has your friendship with Jesus made you a better person?

EUCHARISTIC LIVING

By participating in the Eucharist, we respond to Jesus' invitation and open ourselves for him to mediate our lives. At Mass we hear Scripture proclaimed, and we eat and drink at the Eucharistic table. Both actions fill us and motivate us with the law of divine love. Then, we are dismissed from Mass and sent out into the world. It is as if we cannot hold within ourselves the love of God we have been shown in Jesus.

When we actively witness to the Good News of salvation in Christ, the prophecy of Jeremiah is fulfilled. God's living law of love, placed in our minds and written in our hearts, is manifested to the world.

 Discuss how participation at Mass deepens your relationship with God in Christ.
How is the law of love manifested in your family, school, and community?

Called into Relationship
Matthew 11:25–30

*T*here are some things in life that we simply cannot do without, for example, that special braided friendship wristband that we always wear, or that cell phone that we seem to always be using, or that portable DVD player that we cannot set down for even one minute, or that friend who is always with us—as if we are joined at the hip! Though it is nice to have all these kind of things, as Catholics the one thing we truly cannot do without is trust and hope in God.

Reading the Word of God

Matthew
11:25–30

In the verses preceding this passage, Jesus criticizes the citizens of Chorazin and Capernaum for their unbelief in the face of his miracles and mighty deeds. Think about the questions below before reading the passage directly from the Bible. Afterwards, record your responses.

To whom does Jesus go for strength?

Whom does Jesus name as accepting and rejecting his message?

In Jesus' day young people grew up fast! At age fourteen some boys began to work. Young girls would, often times, be promised to marriage and sometimes married to a suitor.

- Society did not consider children younger than age fourteen as important. Children were loved and cherished by their families, but they were considered socially insignificant.

- People would not have considered a child wise, mature, or the recipient of special knowledge, much less as the Son of God from heaven.

AS A CHILD

Jesus is not saying that believers arrive at acceptance of his message and its significance because they are reduced to childish behavior. Being *childish* is not the same thing as being *childlike*. For a young child, all the world is new and fresh, a place of wonder and delight to be explored.

Faith opens a whole new world for us in wonder and delight. *Who in your life exemplifies childlike acceptance of faith?*

Spend a few minutes in a small group focusing more on the second part of this passage, Matthew 11:28—30.

 Discuss what invitation Jesus makes and to whom.

THE AUTHORITATIVE GUIDE

Chapters 5 through 7 of Matthew's Gospel present the core of Jesus' teaching. While this teaching builds on the old covenant, Jesus stretches beyond the limits of the old covenant. He sets himself up as the authoritative interpreter of the old covenant (Matthew 5:22, 28, 32, 34, 39, 44). No rabbi of Jesus' time would do this. Rabbis would never consider themselves above the old covenant or authoritative interpreters of it.

Jesus promises us that if we accept him as the authoritative figure in our lives, direction and guidance will be ours. Trials and difficulties may remain, but following Jesus will help us better navigate life.

What family members, friends, and teachers help guide you?

A yoke was a wooden bar that hitched together a team of oxen. Farmers would use the guide straps of the yoke to direct the oxen as the farmers plowed the fields.

- In Old Testament days, the prophets used the image of the yoke to signify obedience to the laws of the covenant.
- In effect, the prophets meant that the people of God were "yoked" to the law—through it they received guidance for the correct direction in life.

Who are people you know whose burdens have been made easier because they accept the authority of Jesus?

COMPLICATIONS MADE SIMPLE

Some people in Jesus' time considered the old covenant burdensome and heavy because of its extensive regulations. Ordinary people often had difficulty observing such a vast number of the laws, sometimes simply because they could not remember them all.

Jesus cuts through all those complications. He preaches a simple double commandment of love of God and neighbor, and he offers himself as the authoritative guide to living that commandment. That is why the yoke of Jesus is easy and his burden light.

Accepting Jesus as the authority may mean rejecting others. *Why?*

Reread Matthew 11:25—27. On the board or on a large piece of newsprint, define the phrase: *meek and humble*. Then, based on your definition, consider what it means to be *meek and humble* in today's world.

MAKING TIME

Jesus calls us to learn from his example of meekness and humility. Believers can be strong and determined. The challenge Jesus presents is for us to follow his example of a *heart* that is meek and humble (Matthew 11:29).

Jesus refers to an internal attitude and a perspective on the world that links with his image of being *childlike*. This attitude and perspective can be cultivated by slowing down and by taking time to pause and reflect on our experiences. Reflection allows us the space within ourselves to savor the good experiences and learn from the bad ones. Pausing from time to time enables us to see the world with awe and wonder.

How much time daily do you spend in quiet prayer or individual reflection?

Would you say that your prayer and reflective moments make you wiser or more childlike, or is it a combination of both? Explain.

EXAMINE YOUR CONSCIENCE

An *examination of conscience* serves to check how we have acted (or failed to act) in loving ways towards God and our neighbor. It requires only honesty and a few minutes at the end of the day. This practice also prepares us for the Sacrament of Reconciliation.

- Find a quiet space away from distractions.
- Ask the Holy Spirit for help.
- Mentally review the day, its major parts, and experiences.
- Ask yourself: Did I live up to the example of Jesus? Did I fail to live up to the example of Jesus?
- Conclude with a prayer of praise to God.

This traditional Catholic practice helps us view our lives through the lens of faith. It exemplifies those who follow Jesus with meekness and humility of heart—those who are not too proud to find new things to learn from each day.

 Reflect on whether you are honest with yourself. Is honesty a burden or a relief? Why do you think an examination of conscience is important before the Sacrament of Reconciliation?

*A*lmost every school has them. Student bodies around the country divide up into factions, or cliques, because of competing interests or outlooks. Each clique has its own name and group members. Because students band together in these groups and sometimes look down on members of other groups, cliques have the potential to harm the unity of a school student body.

Reading the Word of God

1 Corinthians
1:10–18

Before you open your Bible, read the questions below. After you read this portion from Paul's first letter to the Corinthians, answer the questions.

The Greek city of Corinth was a bustling commercial port and a crossroads for different peoples, cultures, and businesses. The community of believers may have been characteristic of the city itself—cosmopolitan, worldly, full of different views and ideas, and greatly diverse.

What is the emotional tone of this passage?

Who does Paul name as the responsible parties for division within the Corinthian Church community?

GROWING PAINS

Paul traveled to Corinth and established the Christian Church there. As the community grew, disagreements began to develop among its members. The community fractured into various groups who claimed their own leaders as more knowledgeable than others.

Would you describe yourself as argumentative? Would others?

Do you think most people get involved in arguments that could be avoided? Why or Why not?

Reread the Scripture selection. Pay particular attention to verses 17 and 18.

 Why are these final verses so important to Paul's argument?

To what singular and unique message does verse 18 refer?

When Paul describes the message of the cross in 1 Corinthians 1:18 as *foolishness*, he presents a paradox. In and of itself, death on a cross would not seem to be a source of wisdom and power. However, Christ's followers know it to be otherwise. To those who do not believe, this message is lost.

WORLDLY WISDOM OUTRANKED

The factions within the Church at Corinth threaten to tear it apart. Paul founded the community and cares about its health, so he argues that only one thing will rally them together—the event that stands above our limited human reasoning and logic. One singular, unique event gives meaning to our faith: the cross of Christ.

Paul notes that the significance of the cross does not necessarily make sense by worldly standards. The world sets standards according to its measures of health, beauty, wealth, and safety. On the other hand, God sets standards according to divine measures of love, self-sacrifice, endless giving, and risk–taking for the sake of truth. From God's perspective, the message of the cross outranks any worldly standard.

 Discuss a time when you took part in a truly important argument about something really critical. How did you get involved? What prompted you to take action?

In the end, did everyone come to an agreement?

THE PULPIT OF THE CROSS

A pulpit is a place from which someone stands and preaches a message. One way to look at Jesus' suffering and death on the cross is to see it as a "pulpit" from which Christ communicates God's message of love and self–sacrifice to us. In this sense, Jesus' three hours on the cross summarize and complete his entire life and earthly ministry.

While on the cross, Jesus "speaks" with the eloquence of heavenly speech. Human wisdom looks weak in comparison to the Good News preached from the pulpit of the cross! The message of those last three hours remains consistent with Jesus' public ministry—a message of peace, forgiveness, love, and reconciliation.

 Reflect quietly on the thoughts that come to you right now. Then, imagine the scene of Jesus' crucifixion and the Lord speaking just to you from the cross. *What does he say that you need to hear?*

MYSTERY

It does seem odd, at first glance, that in his argument to the factions at Corinth, Paul would put together the ideas of power and the cross. Someone who has been nailed to a cross doesn't have much power. The crucified is a victim who has been overtaken by others. It looks like a dead end with no hope in sight.

The fact that new life arises from this dead end is the deepest mystery of our faith. Our call to follow Christ comes directly from the cross because the cross represents God's answer to all the world's perplexing and agonizing riddles.

What are the experiences that plague us, hurt us, or beat us down?

What are the dead ends in life people experience? How can faith in Jesus turn those around?

Jesus faced a horrifying end, but God the Father turned that terrible reality into a great good. This mystery of Jesus draws us onward and calls to us. United by faith in his death, may all believers share in Christ's glorious Resurrection!

MOTIVATION

Paul's argument to the community at Corinth puts forward the image of the cross as a sign of God's un-selfish love for us. The love of Christ compels us to follow.

Once the Corinthian community received Paul's letter, they must have talked about it. They would have evaluated their shortcomings and rivalries in the light of the cross. All of us measure our following of Christ by his self–sacrificing love. When we allow the cross to be our motivation, our pride is conquered and our weakness is turned to strength.

Are there rivalries and divisions between yourself and others? Are members of your family alienated? How does this experience make it difficult to follow Jesus?

What steps can you take to eliminate those rivalries and divisions? If you cannot address them right now, you can pray to the Crucified Jesus for strength—and allow your "answer" for the time being to remain within the mystery of the cross.

Called to Follow Jesus

Matthew 8:16–27

When you were younger, you and your friends probably "made believe" and pretended to be cowboys, police officers, teachers, soldiers, racecar drivers, nurses, or many others. Little children pretend to be adults by mimicking adult professionals and adult ways of life. Students just out of college sometimes spend a few years trying out various professions or jobs until they find the one that suits them. At some point, either by deliberate action or by passive inaction, all people choose a particular path to follow.

Reading the Word of God

Matthew
8:16–27

This passage picks up the narrative in mid-stream. The "they" in verse 16 is unclear and refers either to townspeople from Capernaum or to Jesus' first, inner circle of disciples. Read the passage and answer the following questions.

There are three distinct scenes or episodes here. Summarize the different kinds of activities in which Jesus engages.

What does Jesus do that is so amazing, and how do his followers react?

The phrase *Son of Man* comes from the Old Testament (Daniel 7:13–14) as a term synonymous with "saints of God." Jesus refers to himself as the Son of Man whenever he talks about his earthly ministry—such as he does here in verse 20—or elsewhere in the Gospels when he predicts his Passion or his future activity as judge at the end times.

AMAZING POWER

Jesus has already been engaged for quite some time in his public ministry. Up to this point, Jesus has been teaching and preaching with great authority. However, now in Matthew's narrative, Jesus performs a series of mighty deeds that further impress his followers and the crowds.

What recent event stopped you cold and had you talking about it for days?

Have you ever experienced a "retelling" of an event that made it sound bigger than it really was? How does that sort of thing happen?

Reread Matthew 8:16–22. Compare and contrast the two men who speak to Jesus in this part of the passage.

The scribe approaches Jesus and asks to become his disciple. The man claims that he will follow Jesus and be a disciple.

For the scribe, discipleship would entail a huge change. Scribes studied the scrolls of the Old Testament. They were knowledgeable in the religious law. This required a personal library and a permanent home in which to put it. The scribe would have to give up his former way of life in order to follow Jesus. We do not know whether or not the scribe actually becomes a disciple because the more important piece of information for us is Jesus' response.

Hyperbole is a figure of speech that exaggerates or overstates the case. For example, you may exclaim, "Stop! You're killing me!" You don't really mean that you are dying—only that you are laughing so hard that it hurts.

 Reflect on the following: Disciples go where Jesus leads. *Where do you think you will end up in life? Does thinking about your future excite you or make you anxious? Why? How is Jesus involved in the direction your life is taking?*

DISCIPLESHIP IS ALWAYS

A follower of Jesus asks if he can go bury his father. Jesus knows that burying a parent is both a loving and religious task, so he uses his response to shock his listeners so that they truly hear what he says.

Jesus employs hyperbole to make a point: nothing should stand in the way of becoming and remaining a disciple. We cannot turn our discipleship on and off depending on our personal needs.

Have there ever been times or situations where you wished you weren't a follower of Jesus? Why?

FOLLOWING JESUS, QUESTIONING THEMSELVES

Jesus takes the initiative, gets in the boat, and Jesus and his disciples begin to cross the sea. A terrible storm blows up out of nowhere and the disciples panic. They plead with Jesus to save them from drowning.

The Lord speaks sharply to the wind and sea. Everything becomes calm, except, perhaps, the disciples themselves!

The storm that hits them is no little thing. The author of the Gospel according to Matthew uses the Greek term *seismo*, which means "earthquake." The weather and the situation, along with Jesus' action, left quite an impression on the disciples.

They no longer fear for their lives, but their agitation is evident. They realize they do not really know Jesus. He has surprised and frightened them with this show of awesome power. Their question about his nature (Matthew 8:27) will not be fully answered until after the Resurrection.

Discuss some of the storms that we experience in life? How does Jesus calm these storms?

A LITTLE IS ENOUGH

Being called to follow Jesus does not happen only in good times or when our lives are moving along reasonably well. Our calling as disciples carries us through difficult, challenging, and stormy times.

Jesus frames his description of the disciples in the boat as a question (Matthew 8:26), but it is also meant as reassurance, especially for us who come later and are now "looking in" at this episode through Scripture. A little bit of faith is enough so that Jesus might act and save us from the storms.

Anything else would be presumption on our part—as if what we have within ourselves, lots of faith, somehow tips the balance and makes Jesus save us. Salvation doesn't depend on us. It's a free gift from Jesus. All it requires on our part is the little bit of faith that acknowledges we can't save ourselves. So we rely on the Lord to lead the way, speak the word, and calm the seas.

If you had to rate the quality of your faith from 1 to 10 (with 10 the highest), how would you rank and why?

Do you think you have enough faith?

*A*n athlete spends her entire formative years preparing for Olympic competition and a chance to win a gold medal. She dedicates all of her time to becoming the best in her field. Some years she performs at the top of her game. Others, she does not. Either way, she keeps the goal in mind. She visualizes it. And as she does so, she continues to hone the skills and abilities that will enable her to achieve her goal. Athletes are not the only ones who work hard striving for a worthy goal or reward set in the future. We all do, in various ways.

Reading the Word of God

Matthew
5:1–16

Before you open your Bible, read the questions below. Then, after you have studied this scripture passage, answer the questions.

What is Jesus doing in this episode?

As a follower of Jesus, what does one have to be or do to receive God's blessings?

Mountains in the Old Testament were frequently the location for important revelations from God — especially, for example, when Moses received the tablets of the divine law. Unlike Moses who receives teaching from heaven, Jesus gives it.

A GUIDE FOR LEARNING

Teachers in Jesus' day sat on a chair or bench while their students sat on the ground in front of them. This arrangement, where the teacher had height over the students, emphasized the important role of the teacher as a guide for students' learning.

Think back on the teachers you have had. *Who have been some of your most effective teachers and why?*

What are the qualities of good teachers?

When a coach spends the last five minutes in the locker room at half-time pumping up the team, that quick pep talk does not negate everything the coach has previously trained the team to do. The coach's talk is meant to motivate and inspire within the framework of his entire coaching.

It is the same with the Beatitudes. They highlight Jesus' teaching and the example of his own life and ministry. Jesus assures us that God blesses those who strive to place their lives in service to kingdom values. He names specific ways that believers strive to realize those values.

The kingdom Jesus talks about is not located in a particular geographical place. Rather, the kingdom has to do with how God is ruler over all creation and how those who believe strive to live under the guidance and dominion of God.

 Reflect on a time when someone gave you a little pep talk before a difficult task or situation. *What was that like, and did it help you?*

FUTURE BLESSINGS

The first and the last Beatitudes are in present tense, but Jesus speaks of all the others in the future tense. We may work hard every day to put the teaching of Jesus into practice. We might not always see the fruit of that in our lives, or in the lives of others. Indeed, some Christians experience persecution and hardship. They look forward, as do we, to a future when all God's sons and daughters will experience his blessing.

Ultimately, the reward of our fidelity to the teaching of Jesus will be granted to us in heaven. Eternal joy and overwhelming beatitude await us. Just because our reward may be put off till heaven, it does not mean that it is not something worth our striving. Good things are worth the waiting, especially heaven.

 What are some things that you strive for now but the reward will be delayed in the future? Does this make the striving any less worth it?

WE ARE EXAMPLES

 Reread Matthew 5:13 – 16. *What two images does Jesus use in this passage?*

These images explain why we put the teaching of Jesus into practice. We do not live his teaching because it will involve a blessing—whether that blessing comes to us now or in the future. We live his teaching because it is good in and of itself. We desire to show others what it means to live as members of the kingdom.

Putting the teaching of Jesus into practice is not simply for our own benefit. Our actions enhance the flavor of life for *others* and illuminate or push back the darkness for *all.*

In small groups review the Beatitudes again. What words catch your attention? How do they help you understand the goals of Christian living?

Spend some time answering these questions and then share your responses with another person.

What are your goals in life right now? How do those goals include Jesus?

AN ATTITUDE

It would be easy to say that this Scripture calls us to give up our possessions and become poor, or, that we must all be meek and never contradict what another tells us. However, this would miss the point of the Beatitudes.

The Beatitudes are first and foremost an attitude that we cultivate in every aspect of our lives, an attitude that says: *God rules.* Our lives are a gift from God, and we are meant to return that gift by striving to live the teachings of Jesus as best we can.

WHERE WE FIND HAPPINESS

The Beatitudes convey to us the essence of Jesus' message. True happiness does not lie in great wealth or power, in human fame or achievement. Our happiness lies in God alone.

Catholics who strive for beatitude or blessedness from God sometimes start their day with a simple ritual gesture. Upon waking up from sleep, the first thing they do is to make the Sign of the Cross and afterwards pray: "Lord, I dedicate this day to you, in all I do and say." The challenge, of course, comes for us then in making that happen throughout our waking hours!

Choose two Beatitudes. *In what ways do you live out these Beatitudes at home, in school, and around your community?*

In what ways do you model Jesus' message for others? How can you be an example to those around you?

*Y*ou tell somebody something. They don't accept your word for it, even when you are simply relating facts. Or something just happened, and you describe it. The information you share is essential for decision-making and a correct response in a situation. They still don't believe you. When the situation later crumbles apart, it would be so easy for you to engage in: I told you so!

Reading the Word of God

Matthew
13:1–23

In this scriptural episode, the crowd is so huge that no one can see or hear Jesus. So he must climb into a boat and speak to people as they stand or sit upon the shoreline. Think about the questions below before reading the scripture passage. Afterwards, record your responses to the questions.

The parables of Jesus are stories taken from nature or common life experiences. They are characterized by metaphor and simile. That is, Jesus makes comparisons with everyday items and situations to help us understand the truths of the kingdom of God. Most of the parables have surprising details that catch our attention, shock us, and draw us to the truth Jesus seeks to impart.

To whom does Jesus address in the parable (Matthew 13:1-9)?

To whom does Jesus direct his explanation of the parable (Matthew 13:11-15)?

On this day, Jesus pronounces another beatitude. What does this beatitude concern?

In your view, what is the most odd or confusing detail found in this parable?

The crowd of Galileans in this parable would immediately relate to the activity Jesus describes in the parable. Galilee is the bread basket for the entire region, where most of the crops are grown. Those who originally heard this parable would relate immediately to the image that Jesus weaves of a farmer who is sowing seed to produce a crop.

MORE POTENT THAN WE EXPECT

In Jesus' day the ineffective methods of planting would yield a meager amount, about fifteen-fold. Using these particular farming methods could never yield crop in the amazing figures Jesus gives. Here lies the surprising detail *and point* of Jesus' first parable on this day of parables. The word of God, the message of Jesus, will yield abundantly because that's the way it is with the kingdom and grace from heaven. God's grace is so potent that it can yield all out of proportion to our human expectation.

 What are some times God has acted in your life or that of a family member or friend beyond expectation or understanding?

Jesus accurately describes the farming methods of his day.

- The sower, or farmer, would first throw seeds on the ground and only afterwards plow it under.
- This differs from the effective, more modern process of plowing furrows, then carefully placing all the seeds into the ground, and finally covering them over with dirt.

REJECTION WON'T STOP GOD

Not everyone embraces the message of Jesus. Not everyone accepts him as Lord and Teacher. Some members of the crowd hear what he has to say, consider his preaching, shrug their shoulders, turn away, and remain indifferent. But those who *do* accept Jesus' word and the message of the kingdom will have an amazing impact on the world—because God's grace works in us and yields one-hundred, sixty, and thirty fold!

The mixture of rejection and acceptance to Jesus' teaching *will* work according to God's plan. It is a plan first hinted at by Isaiah the prophet whom Jesus quotes (Matthew 13:14-15) as Jesus further explains the meaning of the parable to the disciples.

 Read again Matthew 13:18 – 23, in which Jesus continues to explain his parable. Discuss with a partner the ways Jesus identified different groups of people with the different settings in which the seed can fall.

Jesus explains that some will reject his teaching. The "evil one" works to turn people away from the Good News. Superficial acceptance prevents some from developing deep roots in Jesus. Worldly concerns and seeking wealth will turn others away from faith. And some will accept Jesus' teaching. Jesus describes these people as "rich soil" who take not only the time to hear his word, but also to "understand" it (Matthew 13:23).

 Reflect on times when you don't understand what the Church teaches or why the Church teaches it. *What do you do to try and better understand it?*

CELEBRATING THE WORD

The first step in hearing and understanding the word is celebrating it. We celebrate the power of God's word when we gather for Mass. We hear God's word from both the Old and New Testaments. The New Testament lies hidden in the Old—and the Old Testament becomes more vivid and clear through the New. In other words, Christ is the heart and fullness of all Scripture, just as he is the center of the entire liturgy and our lives.

But hearing and celebrating Scripture is only the first step in understanding it. Once we understand Scripture, the better we can carry the mystery of Christ forward into our lives.

How do you make Scripture a part of your life?

In what ways do you try to understand God's word and act on it in your daily life?

GROWING TOGETHER TO UNDERSTAND MYSTERY

We will never fully understand the mystery of God, but that does not mean God remains totally beyond us. In fact, God reveals himself in Christ to bring us closer to his mystery. Your study of Scripture right now is an attempt to understand the mystery to which Christ draws us.

Understanding Scripture is an example of how we can apply the message and Jesus' explanation of this parable. This process of study could be done individually. Notice, Jesus explains the parable to his disciples, as a group. He addresses the "you" in Matthew 13:11 to them all. What one individual might miss, others may see, and therefore, the understanding of all is deepened.

Have you ever been a part of a study group? How has that helped you?

How do you feel about those who do not accept the message of Jesus? How might we, as a group of Christian believers, be a blessing, a beatitude for those who do not accept Jesus?

Called to Believe

Mark 8:27–38

We constantly move from place to place. Cars, buses, subways, bikes, or our own feet get us where we need to be. Each day requires many physical movements. Developing as a person is also movement, but of a different kind. Becoming a better student, teammate, or artist requires a different sort of "transportation." Becoming the person we want to be may involve a change of geography, for example, in our choice of a college far from home. Whether we stay close to home or not, becoming the person we want to be involves an interior journey of discovery and personal acceptance.

Reading the Word of God

Mark
8:27–38

 Typically the disciple has the role of asking questions of the teacher. The teacher then definitively answers. In this fashion, the disciple receives the teacher's wisdom and knowledge. In this conversation with his disciples, Jesus turns the tables on them.

This scriptural episode sits in the very middle of the Gospel according to Mark. Up to this point, Jesus has been engaged in his public ministry, teaching and healing the people. The writing style of the author is almost breathless and hurried, mirroring the fact that Jesus never stops or rests. Now, however, Jesus pauses and engages his disciples in a critical conversation.

This passage has three distinct sections. Before you read it, consider the questions below. After you have read it, answer the questions.

What does Jesus ask his followers?

How does Peter respond to Jesus in verses 27–30 and verses 32–33?

INTERIOR TRAVEL

The public ministry of Jesus has taken the disciples to the area around Caesarea Philippi—currently the northern tip of Israel. They will end up in Jerusalem. On the way, they will travel throughout Israel. The physical journey serves as the backdrop for the interior journey that forms the disciples as the followers of Jesus.

Why does something as simple as a field-trip or something as momentous as leaving home for a summer program abroad have an impact on us?

Going Deeper into the Word of God

Peter proclaims Jesus as the Messiah, the one for whom Israel has been waiting. However, most of the people, Peter among them, expected that the prophesized Messiah would restore the kingship of David and, therefore, throw out the occupying army of the Roman Empire.

Instead, Jesus reveals that the leaders will reject him and that he will suffer and die. Peter cannot abide such talk, so he tries to engage Jesus in private conversation. Jesus brings in the other disciples, uses this as a teaching moment, and corrects those mistaken ideas about the role of the Messiah.

 Reflect on the following: Jesus' disciples misunderstood the meaning of who he was. *How does it feel to be misunderstood, and do you correct people who say you are one kind of person when you are actually another?*

THE ROUTE TO EVERLASTING LIFE

 Reread Mark 8:34–38. *What does Jesus teach about the requirements of discipleship?*

The way of Jesus—and the way of those who wish to follow as his disciples—will be the way of the cross. Jesus calls his disciples to deny themselves and give up any expectation of benefit. In fact, disciples must be prepared to carry their own cross. The cross will lead to gaining what is most important: everlasting life.

Jesus could be referring to an actual physical death by persecution for his followers, or his talk of "picking up one's cross" might also be figurative. *What are the figurative crosses in life for us believers?*

 Roman authorities in the time of Jesus reserved crucifixion only for those individuals considered a threat to the empire, such as political revolutionaries. Those who were to be executed had to carry the cross-beam to the place of execution as a further object lesson for the bystanders— don't challenge the authority of Rome and the emperor.

A TURNING POINT

Jesus doesn't just turn the tables on his disciples with his question and this teaching about his impending suffering, dying, and rising. This conversation represents a turning point for the disciples where they learn from Jesus the path and the implications of discipleship.

Jesus does not hide the difficulties involved. He is very upfront about the cross, and he makes clear this is the *only* way. The disciples cannot hide or ignore the course Jesus sets before them.

This is an important turning point. The disciples must set aside their assumptions about Jesus as Messiah and trust in his startling revelation about the cross. They have to believe what he is saying and embrace that belief.

The very term Jesus uses to describe his follower, a disciple, implies that the task of the disciple is to be disciplined. Notice the command Jesus gives Peter (Mark 8:33). The place of the disciple is to "get behind," that is, to follow where the teacher leads. This will require Peter—and by extension, every disciple—to make the internal changes necessary to follow. Following Jesus to a difficult place, the cross, requires discipline.

 Discuss and identify, in small groups, the qualities of a person that make him or her disciplined. List those qualities on newsprint and place them around the room so all can see. *What role do these qualities have in the Christian life?*

LEARNING MEANS STUMBLING

Here in this scriptural episode and throughout his Gospel account, the author of Mark presents the disciples as simply not getting it. They remain obtuse, blinded to the implications of Jesus' message and mission.

In short, they are human. They are very much like us. Just because the original disciples see Jesus up close and personal, it does not mean they have more of an advantage than we do. We all stumble in our following. There are times when we don't "get it."

What in Jesus' message and mission do you sometimes "not get"?

In those instances, how do you come to understand the true meaning of Jesus' words? How do you change your behavior to show your understanding?

What are some ways that disciples of Jesus stumble today?

How can the Church community help us when we stumble or help us avoid stumbling in the first place?

Fear is a natural reaction to someone or something that threatens us. The fear of death or grave injury typically causes people to run out of a burning building. Obviously, it is sometimes very appropriate to give in to fear. On the other hand, sometimes we must set aside or ignore fear. For instance, the same normal reaction of fear to a fire must be overcome by a firefighter in order to run inside that same building to save people.

Reading the Word of God

Mark
16:1–8

Before you read this passage, read the questions below. After you have studied this Scripture, respond to the questions.

What are the women preparing to do?

The young man inside the tomb tells the women a number of things. *What are those things, and which one do you think is the most significant? Why?*

Each of the Gospels describes differently the messenger(s) at the empty tomb.

- In the Gospel according to Mark, we read of a young man wearing a white robe.
- In the Gospel according to Matthew, we learn of the angel of the Lord whose "clothing was white as snow" (Matthew 28:3).
- In the Gospel according to Luke, we find that "two men in dazzling garments" spoke to the women (Luke 24:4).
- In the Gospel according to John, we read that "two angels in white" sat at the tomb and spoke to Mary Magdalene (John 20:12).

A SHORT ENDING

The Gospel according to Mark culminates with the message in this passage. Everything that has happened leads us to this point. Most Scripture experts agree that the Gospel originally ended with verse 8, and someone added verses 9 through 20 later.

Read this passage again, paying particular attention to verses 7 and 8.

Do you think that the author concludes with a curious ending? Why or why not?

The young man at the tomb commands the women to tell the other disciples that the Risen Lord will meet them in Galilee. But the women leave the tomb and say nothing to anyone. We read in the Gospel according to Mark that they are afraid. Fear conquers them, and they keep silent when they should be shouting the message of the Resurrection from the rooftops. This Gospel account presents an equality of faults among Jesus' followers. Both men and women fall short of the amazing Good News given to us in Christ.

 Reflect on a time you may have failed at something important or did not complete a task to your best ability. *How did you feel? Were you able to overcome that failure? Why or why not?*

LACK OF ACTION

This scriptural episode does not end in a very positive or upbeat way. The women have received world-shaking news, but they do nothing about it.

The reaction of the women, at first glance, is depressing and disappointing. Perhaps, the news of the Resurrection overwhelms them, or it seems beyond belief. Maybe their imaginations cannot grasp what the man says, and they are confused. Or it simply could be that they are afraid to report what they have seen and heard at the tomb because they think the disciples will ridicule them.

In spite of the women remaining silent, great good does result—someone does *eventually* proclaim the Good News. Otherwise, we modern day believers would not exist!

MEETING THE LORD

 This Gospel of Mark begins and ends similarly. In both cases, someone announces an upcoming encounter with Jesus, the Messiah and Son of God. Read Mark 1:1–3, 7–8 and Mark 16:5–7. *What are the similarities between the two passages?*

The Gospel writer quotes the prophet Isaiah at the outset. Believers should "prepare the way of the Lord," for he is coming. At the tomb, the women hear that Jesus will meet the disciples; they will see him in Galilee. The final command of the young man parallels the ancient prophecy (Isaiah 42:16) in that the men disciples who have been just as blind and stumbling as the women will soon "see" the Risen Lord.

Fear and human limitations will sometimes constrain our discipleship. But God will take the initiative and restore us, no matter how often we fail. Forgiveness, healing, and life-changing good news will be our inheritance.

 Have you ever been totally surprised by God with good news—such that you are left speechless? Describe the experience.

Do you truly believe that God forgives you for sometimes failing to live up to the Good News of the Resurrection?

Applying the Word of God to our Lives

IN OUR HOMES AND LIVES

The promised encounter with the Risen Lord will not take place somewhere out of the ordinary. Even though it is surprising and awesome, the message given to the women at the empty tomb clearly indicates that Christ will meet the disciples in Galilee, where they grew up—their home.

Consider this promise and the following questions.

> *What is the most needed gift that the Risen Christ could bring to your home?*

> *How can your family share the Good News of Jesus with others?*

At Baptism and Confirmation, the Holy Spirit blesses us with seven gifts. We are strengthened with these gifts as we participate in the Eucharist and live out our faith.

Wisdom
Understanding
Counsel
Fortitude
Knowledge
Piety
Wonder or Awe, also known as fear of the Lord.

IN WONDER AND AWE

To be in the presence of God is not easy. God loves us and is close to us, yes. However, God remains far above us, awesome and powerful. If we were to see God face-to-face, our reaction might well be that of Moses, that is, we would cover our eyes (Exodus 3:6). Knowing our shortcomings, we might tremble before the holiness, the beauty, and the goodness of the Risen Christ. God does not love us any less for our fear and trembling.

Break into small groups and review the most important points about Mark 16:1–8. Then answer the questions below.

> *If you were the "young man" in the tomb talking to the women, what would you have said to them?*

> *As a class, compare these messages to the message contained in Mark 16:6–7.*

> *Which one do you find more compelling and why?*

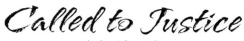

Called to Justice
Luke 19:1–10

Sometimes we can be much too critical of others, and at times our words or actions are overly judgmental. Behaving in this way can lead to making jokes about others by teasing people about their looks, their grades, or their families. Being critical and judgmental tends to isolate others, making them feel like unwelcome outcasts. Limiting someone to the labels we have created for him or her denies him or her the respect and acknowledgment of human dignity that come from being made in God's image.

Reading the Word of God

Luke 19:1–10

Before you read this particular passage, familiarize yourself with the questions below. Once you have read and studied this Scripture, respond to the questions.

Where does Jesus find Zacchaeus, and why is Zacchaeus there?

What two things does Zacchaeus promise as Jesus visits with him?

In the days of Zacchaeus, tax collectors functioned independently of Rome.

• The government did not pay agents a salary for their work in collecting taxes.
• Rome set the tax, and those who collected it added more to the amount for themselves. This additional amount depended on the whim of the agent.
• No one dared to argue with the tax collector or refuse to pay. If so, the agent would simply report them to the Roman soldiers who would then imprison them on the word of the agent.

IN NEED OF HELP

The entire preceding chapter in Luke leads up to this scriptural episode. Luke 18 presents a gallery of people who are desperate for God's help: the widow, the unnamed tax collector (not Zacchaeus), children, and the blind beggar. Zacchaeus may not know it fully, but he needs God's help, too.

Midway through the preceding chapter of The Gospel according to Luke, a rich man expresses his desire to live in a way such that he will inherit everlasting life (Luke 18:18–23). Jesus tells him to give away his wealth to the poor and follow as a disciple. He reacts with sadness, for he cannot detach himself from his riches. Zacchaeus offers us a contrast. He exemplifies the proper attitude toward wealth.

Why do you think Zacchaeus needs God's help?

In what ways do you need God's help?

STEREOTYPED IMAGE

This Gospel passage describes Zacchaeus as the chief tax collector for the region. He has extreme wealth because he receives a percentage from all the other tax agents in the area who work for him.

Because Rome is a foreign occupying force, subjugating Israel, the people see the tax collectors as not only extortionists, but as vile collaborators, helping godless pagans against their fellow Jews. He is not engaged in upright, honorable activity—in that sense, the crowd is right. However, God alone judges sin. In the end, we all are sinners, to one extent or another.

Who are the people in today's society that engage in certain activities, such that others immediately label them as "sinners?"

What happens when you replace Zacchaeus with a modern day sinner? Do you look upon this encounter with Jesus differently as a result?

UNEXPECTED BEHAVIOR

Jesus overlooks the very real sins of Zacchaeus. However, this does not mean that the sins don't exist. It simply means that Jesus takes the first step toward him. Jesus initiates the encounter with someone the crowd believes unworthy.

This gracious and merciful stance frees Zacchaeus from the trap into which he himself has fallen. Because of the social isolation he experiences, he has probably seen himself as others do. He believes himself to be worthless. Therefore, he continues to act in a shady, underhanded way—why try to be good if people won't see beyond your past!

At the same time that Jesus' initiative frees Zacchaeus, the crowd is challenged to free itself from its labeling of the tax collector. Jesus does not deny the reality that is the basis for the crowd's reaction. He is, in effect, proclaiming that God's grace is always available for us to change, to grow and become better, to live up to our true status as beloved sons and daughters in faith.

Zacchaeus experiences the mercy of God through his encounter with Jesus. Zacchaeus's resulting joy becomes apparent as he responds. He gives half of his possessions to the poor. He makes four-fold restitution to those he has extorted. Zacchaeus' response is almost as extravagant as Jesus' initiative toward him.

Reflect on anything in your life that might lead you to think you are not worthy of God's grace. In what ways can you respond to Jesus' offer to change and grow?

Break into small groups of three or four and have someone slowly reread the passage aloud. Concentrate on the sequence of events. Then answer the questions below.

What did Zacchaeus do in order for Jesus to act as he did?

Why do you think that action of Zacchaeus is important?

GOD ACTS, WE RESPOND

God gives his grace freely, even to Zacchaeus. Despite his work practices, Zacchaeus is ready to hear the Good News Jesus shares: God's love and mercy are already ours. For that grace to work within us, we must be properly disposed to cooperate with it.

Once again, in your small group, look over the scripture passage. Jesus speaks a significant word twice. *What is that word? What does that word convey?*

On the one hand, we are not meant to dwell upon the sins of our past or to delay until tomorrow to respond to God's grace. Salvation comes to us here and now, in Christ. It is a grace that is always available to us in the present moment. It is a gift offered to us right now. By visiting and speaking with Zacchaeus, Jesus affirmed the potential for goodness that lay within Zacchaeus as a child of God.

How can Christians your age show they are responding to God's love and mercy by the things they say and do at home and in school?

How can you affirm the goodness in others?

Simeon Stylites, who died in 459, was a monk who desired to give up all comfort, devoting himself to prayer, fasting, and reflection. He resided atop a pillar, upon which a platform had been built, the first one being nine feet high. As the crowds seeking his spiritual advice grew, he had his pillar made taller, to about fifty feet. Later, other monks followed this unusual practice.

Most people love stories. When stories are told right or when they are written with colorful details and a sharp plot line, they engage us. It is almost as if we are brought into the story itself—because we can relate, because we can see ourselves in it, because our imaginations are fired up or our consciences are pushed to a new level of awareness.

Reading the Word of God

Luke
10:25–37

Read this selection in your Bible. Afterwards respond to the questions.

There are two main parts to this scriptural passage. Briefly describe them.

Looking at these two parts in the most general sort of way, how do they differ?

Is the attitude of the scholar of the law toward Jesus friendly or hostile? Why or why not?

Given the way Jesus uses the parable to teach the scholar, we can presume that the man in the ditch is Jewish. The priest and Levite certainly are—they are religious functionaries who serve in the Temple in Jerusalem. It is the Samaritan, therefore, who sticks out—he is *not* Jewish.

TURNING THE TABLES

The dialogue with Jesus does not satisfy the scholar of the law. So he asks Jesus another question that requires an interpretation on Jesus' part. The scholar tries to put Jesus on the spot: define *neighbor*. Jesus does not offer an interpretation. Instead, he tells a story. The story turns the question about *neighbor* back on the scholar and confronts him with an uncomfortable truth!

What questions would you have asked Jesus about the commandments or how to live a life of justice?

On its surface, the parable of the Good Samaritan evokes images of violation and deadly threats. We can imagine what the man in the ditch looks like, beaten to within an inch of his life, left to die. This image is powerful enough.

But when we go deeper into the cultural context, the parable becomes even more powerful. The man who stopped to help comes from Samaria, a region that has its roots in Judaism. People in this region follow the same Hebrew religious law as Israel, but they no longer acknowledge all of the rituals associated with Temple worship in Jerusalem. Therefore, most Jewish people in Galilee consider Samaritans traitors to true faith. It is the traitor, the heretic, the despised and hated Samaritan, who helps the Jewish victim left half-dead in the ditch.

 In groups, read again the parable from Luke. *How does Jesus describe the priest, Levite, and Samartian, and their actions? What do you think the scholar must have thought as he listened?*

 Discuss the following: *If you were to retell this parable today, who would replace the Jewish priest, Levite, and victim? Who would be the Samaritan?*

THEY SHOW NO INTEREST

The outrageous behavior of the Temple priest and Levite does not rest in the fact that they do not help the man in the ditch. Given their religious functions, they must obey the religious law which forbids them contact with a dead body—unless it is a family member (Leviticus 21:1-3). Since the body in the ditch is not a relative, they continue on their way.

However, Jesus presents the priest and the Levite as utterly indifferent to the victim of violence. They don't take the time to even get a little closer and check to see if the man is moving, breathing, or moaning. They both pass by on the other side.

They cannot be bothered by this tragic situation. *That's* the outrage. They are too busy or too consumed with themselves to take the time and effort to even check on the man. Instead, the foreigner, the hated Samaritan, stops and helps, putting himself at risk. The robbers may be hiding, looking for just such a compassionate person as the Samaritan. And yet, he gets involved.

Priests in Jesus' day served for specified amounts of time in Jerusalem, making sacrifices at the altar in the Temple. After they completed their time of service, they would return home to their families. Presumably this is where the priest is heading. Levites also worked within the Temple precincts as door-keepers and minor functionaries.

Why don't people get involved when there are accidents or when someone is hurt?

How is this similar to or different than the way people reacted in the time of Jesus?

Applying the Word of God to our Lives

With the Parable of the Good Samaritan, Jesus teaches us that the kingdom of God removes boundaries and divisions among peoples. All are one. In the kingdom of God, the one who in this world was formerly my enemy is now my neighbor.

To Jesus' Jewish listeners, this would be almost scandalous. To them, there is no such thing as a "good" Samaritan. At worst, Samaritans are the enemy. At best, they are misguided, sinful people.

The conclusion is inescapable. The scholar must answer Jesus: the neighbor is the one who acts with mercy. Compassion reveals the face of my neighbor.

 In smalls groups, identify those that society might consider "enemies" or "opponents" and list them on large pieces of newsprint. Hang the newsprint around the room. Have one of the groups then enact the parable, this time using one of the"enemies" listed on the newsprint in place of the "Samaritan."

How do you feel about the parable now?

MERCY

This parable challenges us because we fall too easily into an "us" and "them" perspective—in almost every arena of life.We may not like to see "them" as capable of mercy. We also may not want to envision ourselves as extending mercy to "them." And yet, Jesus commands us: *Go and do likewise.*

Given this teaching of Jesus, is there ever a time or situation when you shouldn't be merciful?

When are some times you have performed a Work of Mercy individually, with your family, your parish, and your class?

In our Catholic tradition, there are specific acts of mercy spelled out as either corporal (physical) or spiritual works.

Corporal Works of Mercy: Feed the hungry. Give drink to the thirsty. Shelter the homeless. Clothe the naked. Care for the sick. Visit prisoners. Bury the dead.

Spiritual Works of Mercy: Share knowledge. Give advice to those who need it. Comfort those who suffer. Be patient with others. Forgive those who hurt you. Give correction to those who need it. Pray for others.

Your friend needs you. Your friend is at the lockers, and people are calling your friend names, taunting your friend. No one else wants to intervene and stand up for your friend. This is the moment when you have to decide whether you will get involved or not. The ties of friendship and loyalty demand the best of you even though it may not be a pleasant outcome. People might start treating you the same way they are treating your friend.

Reading the Word of God

John
11:1–44

 Before you read this Scripture, be aware of the following questions. Once you have read the passage, respond to the questions.

Some biblical scholars think that another author wrote chapter 11 as an addendum to the original text of the Gospel according to John. This certainly would explain the curious reference in verse 2 about Mary and the anointing, written in the past tense—even though the event will not occur until chapter 12.

There are four main characters in this episode. *Who are they?*

What does Jesus command at the very end and why?

SETTING THE STAGE

This is the longest continuous narrative section in the fourth Gospel, aside from the Passion. This scriptural episode sets the stage for the Passion and explains why the authorities will set in motion the arrest, trial, and execution of Jesus. They are angry at Jesus' sign, the miracle, at Bethany.

What is the overall emotional tone in this scriptural episode?

If you had to pick a piece of music that corresponds to this episode, what would it be?

Jesus loves Martha, Mary, and Lazarus. It seems odd that upon hearing that Lazarus is seriously ill, Jesus waits two days to respond to the sisters request. This does not look like love. Usually, we respond immediately—or as quickly as we can—to the pleas of our loved ones who are in life-threatening situations.

However, Jesus sees this situation from the larger perspective. He knows the sign that he will perform—raising Lazarus from the dead—can only take place if he waits—so that his friend is first dead.

Jesus cares deeply about Lazarus, Martha, and Mary. But through the awesome sign that will take place, the illness of Lazarus and his death will bring into undeniable focus the power and the glory of God shining through Jesus.

TAKING A STAND

The disciples warn Jesus that returning to Bethany may mean big trouble. Some of the people have already tried to kill Jesus by stoning him because he claimed complete oneness with God. Martha and Mary's request will require Jesus to go public again.

Jesus takes that risk and makes a stand. He does so not simply because he desires to work the greatest of his signs, but because he loves Martha, Mary, and Lazarus. They are among his closest of friends, and they symbolize the love Jesus has for all of us. We are his friends, too, by faith.

 Discuss with a partner the people in your life with or for whom you would take a stand and risk everything.

LIFE MEANS DEATH

 Reread John 11:28–44. Think about what Mary says to Jesus and what the other Jews gathered say. How does Jesus respond?

Jesus arrives at the tomb of Lazarus, and his emotion is so evident that the evangelist comments on it: Jesus weeps. Jesus displays human emotion at the death of a friend. He also shows his divine anger. The original Greek for "perturbed and deeply troubled" (John 11:33) cannot be easily translated into English. Jesus' guts are in turmoil; he is furiously angry that human beings die and angry at the effect of original sin, which eventually places all people in a tomb. His entire life and mission comes down to this: to save us *all* from the great enemy. He comes to deliver us from the ultimate effect of sin, which is estrangement from God and everlasting death.

But the price of raising Lazarus from the tomb will be Jesus' own death on the cross (John 11:45–53). The powerful sign of the raising of Lazarus will prompt the authorities to plot Jesus' arrest and execution. Life for Lazarus means death for Jesus. The love that Jesus has for Lazarus and for all of us takes him to the cross—and beyond.

What are the small sacrifices you make daily or weekly for those you love? What sacrifices do they make for you? Is there anything you wouldn't sacrifice for those you love?

Jesus weeps for us all. His great love for us fuels the miracle of raising Lazarus, this sign of God's power. Those who believe will not have to suffer eternal death. We will rise at the word of command from Christ. That word of life, that command, resounds even now!

This scripture passage, therefore, represents good news to us here and now because there are all sorts of "tombs" that seek to claim us. People experience a variety of tombs in this world that prevent them from living fully and well.

 Consider the following in small groups: *What are the tombs in everyday living that sap the life right out of us? How can we help those who find themselves trapped in these sorts of "tombs"?*

FRIENDS OF JESUS

Those who believe in Christ, those who are counted among his friends, try to follow his example. We stand up for one another by seeking that which will promote life in every situation. We help protect and defend one another against the sinfulness that seeks to pull us down. We work for justice so that all people have their basic human rights met.

For example, St. Thomas More, the chancellor of England, took a stand to uphold the papacy and the Roman Catholic Church, which put him at odds with King Henry VIII. Thomas did this, interestingly, because he believed it was in the best interests of the king, who had been his friend. The king, however, imprisoned Thomas, and when the chancellor could not be convinced to break with the Church, he was beheaded on July 6, 1535.

Who are the people in the news who take a stand against evil and confront the "tombs" of this world?

What stands can you take in your neighborhood or local community to promote justice?

A teammate rips down the netting from a basketball hoop after winning a tournament. A high school teenager gets a set of car keys from his parents after passing the driver's test. A husband carries his new bride over the threshold into their new house. All of these are symbolic moments that convey a meaning deeper than the surface level. The netting is not being stolen; it's a trophy. The key does not simply enable ignition; it is freedom. The bride's leg is not broken; both bride and groom are beginning a new life together.

Reading the Word of God

John
13:1–15

Before you read this scripture passage, familiarize yourself with the questions below. After reading from your Bible, answer the questions.

After his actions, Jesus reclines again at table. In Jesus' day throughout the entire Roman Empire, the men would lay on their sides, on couches to eat.

Who is confused by the action of Jesus?

How is his confusion resolved?

A DIFFERENT PERSPECTIVE

This passage starts the Last Supper section in the Gospel according to John. In place of the words that institute the Eucharist—as given in the Gospels according to Matthew, Mark, and Luke—here Jesus performs a humbling act of service for his disciples.

Why do you think Jesus' behavior was so surprising?

In what other ways did Jesus provide his first disciples a model for living?

The disciples show surprise and perhaps, at first, revulsion that Jesus himself performs this service for them. Jesus is their teacher and master. Obviously, he is trying to teach them something by this humbling behavior. However, they cannot wrap their minds around the image of their master assuming the job of the lowliest slave.

 Discuss jobs or roles that some consider lowly or humiliating today. *Whom do people look down upon in our society because of the type of job they hold?*

BAPTISMAL SYMBOLISM

Peter recoils in disgust. He will not let the master wash his feet. However, Jesus explains why this is necessary: without this washing, Peter will not have any claim over the inheritance that Jesus will leave his followers.

This is not a worldly inheritance, but the heavenly reward that awaits all believers. As such, this action of washing symbolizes our Baptism. This may be why Jesus uses the word "bathed" and also mentioned that this washing need be done only once to achieve cleanliness. It is also something that Peter will only fully understand later, as the Church develops and grows and as the sacraments instituted by Christ evolve.

In Jesus' time feet tended to become very dusty and dirty because most roads were not paved.

- People's sandals did not adequately protect their skin from getting gritty and messy.
- When guests arrived for supper, their host usually provided a servant who washed and sometimes scented their feet.
- Only the lowest slave of them all performed this foot-washing service in the household. It was demeaning for the slave.

LOVE THAT LASTS, LOVE THAT ACTS

As this episode unfolds, the evangelist writes that Jesus is aware that his hour has come. The cross looms before him, and he does not turn away from self-sacrifice. Jesus will die for us, but before he does, he provides a powerful example of the type of loving ministry envisioned by God's kingdom.

The washing of feet goes against social convention. It overturns expected modes of conduct. In the kingdom of God, masters become servants, and, in turn, servants become leaders. The kingdom of God subverts the accepted social order and the accepted practices of this world. This is the radical love that will endure. This is the love that will empower our activity to promote the kingdom—a love that overturns worldly expectations.

Radical love also characterizes all those who exercise authority among God's people. Those who will lead the community of faith will follow the example of Jesus and become servant leaders. Leaders of the Christian community will take action to sacrifice themselves in love as does Jesus.

Who are the people who best teach you through their loving example of Christian service?

Do you feel that you follow their example?

Break into small groups and reread this scripture passage, paying particular attention to verses 12–15. Then discuss the following questions in your small group.

How do you understand the significance of your own Baptism? How does Baptism change you for the better in this world, in anticipation of heaven?

How does Baptism affect your life of faith now?

THE POWER OF SAINTLY LOVE

The saints provide example after example of taking the teaching and the example of Jesus to heart. Many saints were strong leaders who energized the faithful, but who did so in a humble, simple way. Blessed Mother Theresa of Calcutta did nothing more than care for the sickest members of society who happened also to be the poorest members of society.

She became famous all over the world for her charity and simple gestures of care: making sure the dying were comfortable, holding their hand, praying with them. This is not the accepted, ordinary mode for a world leader.

Mother Theresa's witness to the faith touched countless thousands. They valued who she was and how she put into practice the teaching of Christ. She was for them an example of the radical love that lasts and acts. For this reason, the Church has declared her a "blessed," someone on the way to sainthood, worthy of honor and acclaim as a Christian hero.

 Discuss whether you believe that the world still needs saints. *Why or why not?*

THE POWER OF SAINTLY LOVE

Among the many titles of the pope—Bishop of Rome, Patriarch of the West, Successor of the Chief of the Apostles, Sovereign of Vatican City State, Supreme Pontiff—the one that best sums up the teaching Jesus imparted by washing the feet of his disciples is Servant of the Servants of God.

The pope, in his role of loving leadership for the Church, serves those who serve.

How is the pope living up to his title as "Servant of the Servants of God"?

In what ways can you be a Servant of God?

Called to Share the Good News

Everyone makes mistakes; it's part of being human. Everyone deserves a second chance. When someone shows a willingness to learn from their past mistakes, other people are more likely to offer them a second, third, or even fourth chance. The opportunity to do better and to correct our mistakes provides hope. Hope is a precious commodity that makes our "today" bearable, even when that day is filled with mistakes. Hope extends to us the possibility that our tomorrows will be better than today.

Reading the Word of God

 Acts
3:1–23

 Preview the questions that follow, then read the passage from your Bible. After reading the Scripture, answer the questions.

Verse 14 refers to Jesus as the Holy and Righteous One. Peter uses a title for God found in the Old Testament and applies it to Jesus. See Leviticus 11:44–45, Psalm 78:4, and Psalm 99:5.

What does Peter say that he does not have?

What does he do for the beggar?

What specific condition does Peter attribute to the crowd and to its leaders, which caused them to initially reject Jesus?

JOHN'S ROLE

While the writer mentions two disciples at the beginning, only one disciple speaks. Peter speaks to the beggar and to the crowd. John remains silent throughout. Nevertheless, John has a critical role. Old Testament Scriptures stipulate that it takes two witnesses to offer proof. John's presence validates the miracle that occurs as well as gives witness to Peter's preaching about the Resurrection of Jesus.

Have you ever been surprised by God or by your faith? Why? What was that like?

Have other people witnessed God's surprising action in your life? How did they respond or react?

Going Deeper into the Word of God

The beggar who cannot walk looks with interest at Peter and John as they pass by, expecting alms from them. He gets something much better than alms. The beggar, so overjoyed at the gift given, attracts attention by his exuberant movements.

Peter preaches to the crowd that has gathered. He explains that this miracle is not a feat of magic; it is not something done by himself or John. Rather, God accomplishes this healing. In doing so, God glorifies Jesus. Through Peter's invocation of the holy name of Jesus, the beggar is restored to full health. The name of Jesus literally means "God saves."

This miracle points to the power of the Son of God. As Peter describes it, Christ is the author of life. Faith in the author of life opens new avenues. The Savior can heal what is broken by sin.

 Quietly reflect on the following: *How often during the week do you call upon Jesus, using his name in prayer and petition before God? How often do you misuse the name of Jesus and curse others?*

The word *apostle* literally means "one who is sent," an official messenger. The disciples Peter and John, along with the others who were gifted with the Holy Spirit, became fearless preachers on behalf of Christ. They are strengthened to do as he commissioned them: to go forth with the message of his Good News.

APOSTOLIC PREACHING

Peter reminds the crowd that they initially rejected Jesus. He offers the members of the crowd and their leaders a second chance, because they acted out of ignorance. They made a grave mistake because they did not understand.

Now, however, they have two very good reasons to be enlightened: the Resurrection of Jesus from the dead witnessed to by Peter and John and the very miracle before their eyes performed in the name of Jesus. Peter's preaching leaves them no choice: he shares the Good News with the crowd, and they must respond.

- The crowd can set aside their misunderstanding of Jesus' identity and mission as they accept the apostolic preaching of Peter.
- Or they can cut themselves off from the blessings assured by all the prophets—blessings fulfilled in Christ.

Those who were once uncertain—abandoning Jesus when he was arrested, denying him, hiding from the authorities—now become fearless apostolic preachers. Peter and the other Apostles are given another chance. Peter is given a new lease on life. A simple fisherman, called and sent by Jesus, is beginning now—along with the other Apostles—to shake up the world.

As a disciple, you, too, are sent forth to share good news with others. How are you being prepared?

How do you see others being prepared to share good news?

The beggar has no idea what is in store for him. Gold and silver are nothing compared to what he actually receives from God through the Apostles.

When we pray to God, sometimes our petition is too grounded in this world. Like the beggar, we cannot see past our immediate needs. It is not as if those needs aren't important. They may very well be. After all, the beggar needs money in order to survive. But the gift he receives is much greater. Restored to health, he no longer needs to beg. He can now work for a living, instead of beg for alms.

 Think about the most important thing you have ever asked from God in prayer. *How did you feel about asking for it?*

GLORIFYING GOD

 Reread Acts 3:1–10. *Where does the healing happen? How does the beggar react? How does the crowd react?*

The beggar responds to this healing with an impromptu dance of praise to God. He knows that Peter and John are instruments through which God has worked this miracle.

Instead of asking for specific things from God, sometimes our prayer can be as simple as invoking the holy name, for example: "Jesus, you are Lord and author of my life, and in your name I will try and share good news this day!"

Whether or not we physically dance in praise of God is not important. Our hearts and spirits can always dance to the glory of the author of life.

A prayer which praises God is called a *doxology*, for example, the end words of the Eucharistic Prayer from Mass: "Through him, with him, in him, in the unity of the Holy Spirit, all glory and honor is yours, almighty Father, for ever and ever. Amen." Another example is the prayer entitled the *Glory to the Father.*

For what or for whom do you give thanks and glory to God?

In what ways can you show God your thanks?

*P*eople identify us by what we do. Young people often spend most of their time in school. Therefore, people consider them students. A lawyer who spends his waking hours defending people in court is known as a defense attorney. Someone who protects the public is known as a police officer. Even when you are not in school, people continue to refer to you as a student. The same goes for the defense attorney and the police officer. No matter whether they see themselves as "poets," or "loving spouses," or whatever else, people still identify them by their profession.

Reading the Word of God

Acts
9:1–22

 Before you pick up your Bible to read this passage, familiarize yourself with the questions below so that you can respond to them after reading this Scripture.

Two other places in Acts of the Apostles (Acts 22:6–16 and 26:9–23) describe the conversion of Saul—who is also known as Paul. Though they differ in some minor details, all three accounts essentially record the same thing. The fact that the author reported this conversion episode three times shows its significance.

What is the name of the follower of Jesus in Damascus who helps Saul?

After Saul is baptized what does he do?

 Saul is trained as a Pharisee and, therefore, is thoroughly conversant with the religious law. He has been commissioned by the High Priest to wipe out the Christian Church, initially known as "the way" of Jesus (Acts 9:2).

Why do you suppose that Christianity was first known as "the way?"

How does the Church in today's world follow the way of Jesus?

The authorities have great concern, and Saul has helped to root out and expose Christians. When Christians begin to leave Jerusalem and go elsewhere, Saul follows. On the way to Damascus, pursuing, ironically, followers of "the way," the risen Christ pursues Saul.

The flashing light which knocks Saul to the ground is certainly dramatic enough. However, to further compound the exciting and mysterious event which initiates his conversion, the voice from heaven identifies itself as from Jesus himself. Even more startling, Jesus then asks why Saul is persecuting Jesus himself.

Jesus does not ask why Saul is persecuting his followers. Jesus identifies himself with his Church. When Saul persecutes the Church he is persecuting Jesus himself. The Church *is* the Body of Christ in the world.

 Reflect on the following: *Have you ever been picked on by others? How did that feel? What do you think it would be like to be persecuted for your religious belief?*

Saul did not change his name to Paul after his conversion.

- He had both an Aramaic name (Saul) and a Latin name (Paul), which was not uncommon for Jews who were also Roman citizens.
- Acts never mentions a name change, and Acts refers to him as Saul after his conversion (Acts 9:22–25; 12:25; 13:1–2).
- However, Saul is also referred to Paul after Acts 13:9.

GOD INTERVENES

Even though the author of Acts tells the story of Paul's conversion in great detail, the true subject of the story is a loving and powerful God who does not remain remote and unconcerned about his people. God intervenes. The Risen Christ takes charge and enters human history in a dramatic fashion to save the early Church.

Paul is not the sole beneficiary of this conversion. The entire Church benefits from it. As zealously as he once persecuted the followers of Jesus, Paul will now defend and promote them as he furthers the mission of Christ in the world. The remainder of this New Testament book details the missionary journeys of Paul as he works tirelessly to build up the Church throughout the Roman Empire.

COMPANIONS ON THE WAY

Even though the Risen Christ intervenes, Saul needs human help. His physical blindness parallels his spiritual blindness. Misguided though he is, he is nonetheless open to God, praying and fasting. But Saul cannot do it on his own. A companion in faith is provided in the person of Ananias.

Ananias lays hands on Saul, an ancient gesture of prayer to call down the Holy Spirit. This laying on of hands removes Saul's physical blindness, and he receives insight into the Christian way. With this new inner sight, Saul gradually begins to assume the role to which God calls him.

Think of a time someone ever helped you with an important insight with regard to yourself or some issue. What was that like?

Applying the Word of God to our Lives

WORKING WITH OUR HESITANCY

At first Ananias hesitates in helping Paul. Ananias fears Saul and judges him by his former activity. He sees Saul as a persecutor of the Church. He cannot see past that former occupation until God commands him to help Saul.

In our own witness to the Good News of Jesus Christ, we may sometimes be afraid. The world is not always our ally in promoting the Christian way. Standing up for our faith, getting involved in the lives of others to actively promote the Church, may lead to our being ridiculed or shunned.

 Reread Acts 3:10–19 with one other member of your group. Together, identify what Ananias actually says to Saul.

Do you agree that what Ananias says is not that involved or complicated? Why or why not?

LORD, I AM NOT WORTHY

At Mass, just before receiving Holy Communion, we acknowledge our limits. Yet, as humans and limited as we are, God's mysterious, powerful, and life-changing presence dwells within us through the reception of the Eucharist.

We may be hesitant and fearful in the face of a sometimes hostile world, yet God works through our human limits to help others come to believe. We are imperfect instruments, like Ananias, transformed by grace to become more effective companions on the Christian way.

What do you think are the ideal qualities of a Christian companion?

Why?

Called to be Church
1 Corinthians 12:12–31

A car without wheels isn't going to be of much use; it won't be going anywhere. Without seats, that same car will be very uncomfortable for its passengers. A steering wheel is also crucial, as would be spark plugs to the proper functioning of that car. If all those separate parts were laying around in a junk yard, we would probably be able to identify them as belonging to a car. However, each individual part does not provide for us the car itself. Only when all the parts are put together, do we have an effective car.

Reading the Word of God

1 Corinthians
12:12–31

The faith community established by St. Paul at Corinth was experiencing some division and conflict. He wrote this letter to urge them to overcome the issues that divided them. Before you read this Scripture, become familiar with the questions below. After reading this passage, answer the questions.

The Greek word used in the New Testament for *church* literally means "those who are called out," such as those who assemble or form a congregation. All of the scripture reflection titles of this book explore various implications of belonging to the Church: as those who cultivate a relationship to God, as followers of Jesus, as those focusing on beatitude living, as those concerned with social justice, and so on.

What sacrament gives us a share in the one Spirit and makes us a member of the One Body of Christ?

Given the entire context of this passage, what do you think is the correct answer to the questions at the end (verses 29–30)?

Going Deeper into the Word of God

Paul uses the metaphor of the human body and applies it to our concept of Church. His use of this image provides crucial insights into the mystery of our being called together as one in Christ.

Baptism forms us anew as members of the Church. We are weak, fragile infants who cannot take care of ourselves, we are mature adults, we are young people finding our way in the world—we are many members, but we share in the same Holy Spirit that builds us up as One Body, the Body of Christ in the world.

We come from different ethnic backgrounds. We have different personalities. We have different strengths and weaknesses. We each have unique personal histories and potential.

 As a group, identify the various ethnic backgrounds from which you come. *Does this variety make you any less of a group?*

DIFFERENT, NOT INDEPENDENT

These differences do not mean that as members of the Church, we are independent. Saint Paul makes the argument that God designs our differences, so that built up together, into the One Body of Christ, we can function effectively to pursue the mission of Jesus in the world.

 Reread verses 18–21. Saint Paul has personified various body parts—the eye, the hand, the head, and the feet—and given them a voice to talk to each other. His point is simple yet profound. The parts of the body work interdependently. They depend on one another, just as we do as members of the Church.

 In small groups, think back to this morning as you began the day and got to this point. *Whom did you rely on to get here and how?*

WEAKER OR STRONGER

Some parts are weaker, yet they are just as important as the stronger parts in contributing to the overall effective functioning of our bodies (1 Corinthians 12:22). Anyone would agree that a poke in the eye hurts a lot more than a poke in the hand. But as sensitive as it is, the eye performs a valuable function for the rest of the body.

In the same way, those who are weaker members of the Church perform a valuable function for the One Body of Christ. The poor and the homeless, for example, evoke in us feelings of compassion that can lead us to assist them and also to change the social conditions in this world so that the causes of poverty and homelessness are minimized.

In what ways are you weaker than others? In what ways are you stronger? How is your contribution important in both cases?

A toothache cannot be confined just to the tooth. The rest of the teeth, the jawbone, and even the whole body feel the ache. Saint Paul applies this analogy to the Body of Christ.

A few members who suffer are reason for the entire Church to suffer. Individual believers who are persecuted or victimized impact the whole Church, who grieves and is in pain along with them.

Pain or joy, grief or comfort—we are individual parts and, at the same time, communal whole—One Body in Christ.

How many ways are you an individual who is also a member of a group?

How do you "function" in those groups?

How can these groups make you a better individual?

NOURISHED AS ONE BODY

Every time you come forward to receive the Eucharist, you do so individually. And yet, at the same time, you come forward as one worshiping community, united in the Lord.

St. Augustine, a bishop in Northern Africa in the fourth century, urged the members of the Church to live the Sacrament of the Eucharist which they shared. He preached to the faithful that they should become what they were eating and drinking at the Eucharist: the meal of the Lord, the saving sacrifice of Christ, God's love set before us.

What personal gifts can you offer to the Church to help accomplish the mission of Christ?

How do you actively cooperate with other members of the Church to live the Eucharist in the world?

*W*e've all seen TV shows or movies depicting courtroom proceedings. An attorney jumps up and appeals to the presiding judge, "Your honor, I object!" Only a limited number and type of objections can be made. The judge rules on the objection. The proceedings then continue, either taking into account the objection or invalidating it. Legal cases proceed according to many such rules and regulations all designed to ensure that the person with the loudest mouth doesn't dominate or that the judge does not improperly favor a particular participant. The proceedings are organized in order that the administration of justice is fair for everyone involved.

Reading the Word of God

Matthew
18:15–35

Before you read this scripture passage, familiarize yourself with the following questions. Afterwards, answer the questions based on the passage from the Bible.

FYI

In this passage, Jesus speaks to Jewish believers. It was a routine matter for Jewish people to avoid contact with ritually "unclean" Gentiles and the despised collaborators with the Roman occupiers, the tax collectors.

In the end, if "your brother" will not listen to you, to a few other witnesses, or to the Church, Jesus says that he should be treated similar to two types of people. What are those two types?

What number (how often) is Peter told to forgive?

This teaching of Jesus deals with how the Church should treat known sinners. Some who sin will fall away from the flock. Jesus addresses this phenomenon in the preceding parable (Matthew 18:10–14). Now he takes up the question of someone who sins and yet continues as a member of the Church.

Why is it important that we receive feedback from others about ourselves and our behavior?

Jesus outlines a simple three-step process for giving feedback to others about their sinning. First, a Church member approaches another member and gives them honest feedback. If that doesn't work, then the one offering feedback should enlist the help of two or three other members who can validate the feedback. If that second step doesn't work, the matter should be referred to the entire congregation. If this last step doesn't succeed, then the faith community should shun the sinner.

Honest feedback regarding our faults can only be effective when it is presented in an orderly, non-emotional manner without making an already tense situation worse. Feedback that doesn't result from lots of reflection or from several sources most likely isn't worth giving.

No one likes to hear about his or her faults, but when it is done in the right spirit, it can be a major help to someone. This teaching of Jesus rests on a vision of the Church and her members as a family, offering an honest assessment of erring behavior, while loving the person to whom the evaluation is being made.

The number with which Jesus answers Peter's question in Matthew 18:22 can be translated as either 77 or 490. In either case, the point is that there are no limits to God's ability to forgive, so there can be no limits on our forgiveness. The numbers themselves refer to Genesis 4:24.

 Discuss the following: *Why do we sometimes hesitate to offer feedback to others? Why does immediate feedback in the heat of the moment usually not work?*

BINDING AND LOOSING SIN

Jesus has the power to forgive sins. In sharing this power with Peter and the other Apostles, Jesus also gives them the authority to reconcile sinners with the Church.

This ministry continues in the Church through the Sacrament of Reconciliation, or Penance. This ministry is vital, for as long as one remains in sin, one is dead— cut off from real, authentic life, separated from holiness and goodness.

Nothing we do is ever simply "between we and God"—faith always includes the community. That is why Jesus gave us the sacraments. Jesus talks of "binding and loosing," meaning that whoever is excluded from communion with the Church is also excluded from communion with God. Whoever is received back into the flock of the Church is also received back by God.

God's loving kindness has no limits. The Church mirrors this infinite mercy. As often as a sinner needs to be reconciled with the Church, this reconciliation is available. Peter asks Jesus how often he must forgive. The number given as an answer simply means: always.

What one word would you use to describe the scripture passages?

Why?

Reread Matthew 18:23–35. In groups discuss and answer the following.

What does Jesus teach in this parable?

If Jesus preached this parable today, how would it be different? Who would the servants and master be?

The unforgiving servant learns nothing at all from the mercy his master shows him. The servant does not offer his fellow servants a similar compassion. Thus, in the end, he must pay a price for his harshness. In the same way, members of the Church must always offer one another mercy and forgiveness, no matter how many times it is needed by those who sin.

THE LORD'S PRAYER

When we pray this prayer, we ask God to extend to us the same forgiveness we extend to others. This reciprocity keeps us honest as we all participate, according to our abilities and our function, in the ministry of reconciliation given to the Church.

In this prayer we remind ourselves that if we are not willing to forgive others, then we should not expect that God will forgive us.

Discuss whether there is any sin too great for God to forgive.

SACRAMENT OF RECONCILIATION

Every parish makes public the times for the celebration of the Sacrament of Reconciliation. Half the struggle against sin is admitting to ourselves that we have sinned. The other half is acknowledging and celebrating the infinite mercy of God, who is always ready to forgive our sins.

If a member of the Church commits a mortal (grave) sin, he or she must first receive the Sacrament of Reconciliation before receiving Holy Communion.

Why is it so difficult for us to admit to another person that we have sinned?

What is the most difficult aspect for you in celebrating the Sacrament of Reconciliation? Why?

What is Revelation?

GOD'S WORD TO US

Christians learn about God's revelation through the Bible, which is God's word recorded by humans, and through Tradition, which is the living and authentic transmission of the teachings of Jesus in the Church. Another name for the Bible is Sacred Scripture. Scripture and Tradition together make up the one source of God's revelation. Scripture forms the basis of Tradition, and Tradition helps the Church correctly interpret Scripture.

The Bible is a collection of seventy-three books, arranged in two major parts. The Old Testament contains forty-six books that deal with the time from the beginning of creation to shortly before the coming of Jesus (approximately two thousand years ago). The New Testament contains twenty-seven books. These books deal with the life, death, and Resurrection of Jesus and the beginnings of the Church. The New Testament together with the Old Testament makes up the Bible.

The Bible is God's word. The Holy Spirit inspired the Bible's human authors to write down the Scriptures. God worked through the talents and abilities of the human writers to reveal the truth about himself. We must be careful, however, of the way we interpret the Bible. If we concentrate only on certain passages, or only on the literal meanings of certain sentences, we can become like the blind men with the elephant. We can get caught up in minor details and lose perspective of the overall message—how much God loves us and wishes to share with us his life of love, peace, and joy.

THE OLD AND NEW TESTAMENTS

Every book in the Bible reveals some truth about God. All seventy-three books of the Bible are inspired, or written with the help of the Holy Spirit. For this reason, the Old Testament and the New Testament are both important. As it is recorded in Paul's Second Letter to Timothy:

All scripture is inspired by God and is useful for teaching, for refutation, for correction, and for training in righteousness, so that everyone who belongs to God may be competent, equipped for every good work.
2 Timothy 3:16

Both the Old Testament and the New Testament contain God's word. They tell us of God's ongoing commitment of love to his people. That is why we believe what Psalm 119:105 says "Your word is a lamp to my feet and a light to my path."

As followers of Jesus, we realize the value of the Old Testament. God chose the Israelites, the descendents of Jacob (also called Israel), to be his chosen people. He made a covenant with the Israelites. In the covenant, he promised the Israelites to be their God, and they promised to be his people. The Old Testament deals with this covenant God made with the Israelites through Moses. The Israelites were not always faithful to this covenant. At times they turned away from his way of love. But he did not turn away from the people. In the fullness of time, he sent a Savior or Messiah, to save people from the power of sin and everlasting death.

The New Testament tells about the coming of the Messiah, Jesus, who was the Father's own Son. The New Testament deals with the new covenant God made through Jesus. The four Gospels occupy a central place in the New Testament and in the entire Bible because they tell about the life, teachings, and saving death and Resurrection of Jesus. Through Jesus, God extended the covenant to all humanity. This new covenant began with Jesus and continues today in his Church. Jesus himself is the fullest revelation of who God is. Jesus is the Word of God, who invited everyone to return to God and his plan of loving goodness.

The Books of the New Testament

THE GOSPELS

Matthew   Mark   Luke   John

Although different in many ways, all the Gospels tell the Good News, which is the meaning of the word Gospel. They present the story of Easter faith rooted in the life, death, and Resurrection of Jesus Christ, the incarnate Son of God. They are not biographies or literal accounts of Jesus' life. Instead, they are faith testimonies that were written in a particular time, language, and culture. Yet the messages contained within these stories are true and timeless. We learn that Jesus is the Son of God who has become man. He is true God and true man. Written by people of faith for people of faith, the Gospels tell of God's kingdom, love, forgiveness of sins, redemption of the human race, and promise of eternal happiness for his faithful people.

The Gospels tell the story of a religious life of people on a spiritual journey. As in all stories, there are major characters, plots, a drama, and a climax. The Evangelists—the Gospel writers Matthew, Mark, Luke, and John—told these stories to uncover what was at the center of the religious encounter of the community with God.

Sometimes the Gospels according to Matthew, Mark, Luke, and John are referred to as the four faces or four portraits of Jesus. They are, in fact, four versions of the same story. Each writer developed a somewhat different perception of Jesus because he wrote his Gospel to benefit the needs of the community for whom he was writing. While each is unique, all helped lead their community of faith on a journey to God.

The Gospels of Matthew, Mark, and Luke are referred to as the synoptic Gospels. The word synoptic is taken from the Latin *syn*, which means "together" and *optic*, which means "seen." This term expresses the idea that these Gospels have a similar vision. The Gospel of John, however, is very different from the synoptic Gospels. Using symbolism and powerful imagery, the Gospel according to John emphasizes the divinity of Jesus.

ACTS OF THE APOSTLES

The Acts of the Apostles is an account of the growth of the Church under the guidance of the Holy Spirit.

- Acts is the second part of the Gospel according to Luke and covers Christian expansion in the Roman world.

- In Acts Luke describes the activity of the early Church, including the preaching of Peter and the Apostles, the growth of the first Christian community, the missionary journeys of Paul, and the Council of Jerusalem. This council emphasized the importance of the leadership of the Apostles and their successors in the Church.

LETTERS

Twenty letters, or epistles, follow the Acts of the Apostles. The letters were written to a Christian community or to individuals, and generally took the form of letter writing in the ancient world. The letters open with a greeting that identifies the sender and recipients, followed by a prayer. The body of the letter generally contains an account of Jesus' life, teachings on how to grow in the Christian life, and advice and encouragement to the community. The letters conclude with a brief personal remark and farewell.

The letters of Paul, or the Pauline letters, are the letters from Romans to Philemon, with the Letter to the Hebrews added at the end. The other seven letters of the New Testament are called the "Catholic Epistles." They are called catholic, or "universal," because they were written to the general public instead of to a specific Christian community.

Romans (Rom)	Titus (Titus)
1 Corinthians (1 Cor)	Philemon (Philem)
2 Corinthians (2 Cor)	Hebrews (Heb)
Galatians (Gal)	James (Jas)
Ephesians (Eph	1 Peter (1 Pet)
Philippians (Phil)	2 Peter (2 Pet)
Colossians (Col)	1 John (1 Jn)
1 Thessalonians (1 Thes)	2 John (2 Jn)
2 Thessalonians (2 Thes)	3 John (3 Jn)
1 Timothy (1 Tm)	Jude (Jude)
2 Timothy (2 Tm)	

REVELATION

The final book in the New Testament, the Revelation to John, offers poetic imagery and challenges the reader to grasp the truth of Jesus.

- The author wrote in the style of apocalyptic literature, a form popular with both Christian and Jewish communities at this time. Apocalyptic means "revealed" or "unveiled."

- Apocalyptic writings reveal secrets of heaven or the future by an angel or the risen Christ. Much of the imagery of Revelation comes from the Old Testament books of Ezekiel, Zechariah, and Daniel.

- The book also contains the symbolism of numbers, colors, and images to hide messages from the Romans, who were actively persecuting the Christians. During this time of crisis, these writings were meant to comfort and give hope to a suffering people. They also exhorted Christians to remain faithful to their mission.

Scripture and Liturgy

Catholics gather to praise and worship God in liturgy, the official public prayer of the Church. The original meaning of the word liturgy was a public work, or a service in the name of or on behalf of the people. In Christian terms, the word liturgy describes the participation of the whole People of God in the work of God. The liturgy consists of the celebration of the sacraments, first and foremost the Eucharist, and the Liturgy of the Hours.

Scripture is integral to how we pray and worship. The celebration of each sacrament includes a Liturgy of the Word. This proclamation of Scripture expresses the meaning of the sacrament and calls those who receive the sacrament to respond in faith.

The Liturgy of the Hours is a prayer that includes psalms and readings and is prayed several times a day as a way to mark time as holy and recall God's saving work in creation. The psalms are an integral part to the Liturgy of the Hours.

THE SEVEN SACRAMENTS

In the sacraments Jesus continues his saving work. During his life Jesus welcomed, fed, healed, and forgave people. Through the sacraments he continues to share God's life and love with his followers. Because the sacraments are founded on the ministry of Jesus and witnessed to in the early Church, we can find Biblical roots for the sacraments.

SACRAMENTS OF INITIATION Three sacraments together complete initation into the Church: Baptism, which begins new life in Christ; Confirmation, which strengthens that life; and, Eucharist, which nourishes that life and transforms the receipent to become more Christ like.
Baptism—John 3:5; Matthew 28:19–20; Romans 6:3–11; Acts 19:1–7
  • Confirmation—Acts 8:14–17, 9:17–19, 19:5; Titus 3:4–8
  • Eucharist—John 6:1–15, 25–71; Matthew 26:26–28; Mark 14:22–25; Luke 22:7–20

SACRAMENTS OF HEALING In the Sacraments of Healing God's forgiveness of sins and healing are given to those suffering physical and spiritual sickness.
  • Reconciliation (Also called the Sacrament of Penance, the Sacrament of Conversion, and the Sacrament of Confession)—John 20:19, 22–23; Mark 1:15, 2:5, 10; Luke 7:48, 15:18
  • Anointing of the Sick—Mark 6:12–13, 16:17–18; Matthew 10:8; James 5:14–15

SACRAMENTS AT THE SERVICE OF COMMUNION In these sacraments, Catholics receive the grace to commit to and serve God and the community.
  • Holy Orders—John 10:36, Acts 1:8, 2:4; 1 Timothy 4:14, 2 Timothy 1:6–7
  • Matrimony—Matthew 19:6; John 2:1–11; 1 Corinthians 7:39; Ephesians 5:31–32

Some Catholic Prayers Found in Scripture

THE LORD'S PRAYER — MATTHEW 6:9–13, LUKE 11:2–4

Our Father, who art in heaven,
hallowed be thy name;
thy kingdom come;
thy will be done on earth as it is in heaven.
Give us this day our daily bread;
and forgive us our trespasses
as we forgive those who trespass against us;
and lead us not into temptation,
but deliver us from evil.
Amen.

HAIL MARY — LUKE 1:28 AND LUKE 1:42

Hail, Mary, full of grace!
The Lord is with you;
blessed are you among women,
and blessed is the fruit of your womb, Jesus.
Holy Mary, Mother of God,
pray for us sinners,
now and at the hour of our death. Amen.

MAGNIFICAT — LUKE 1:46–55

My soul proclaims the greatness of the Lord,
my spirit rejoices in God my Savior
for he has looked with favor on his lowly servant.
From this day all generations will call me blessed:
the Almighty has done great things for me,
and holy is his Name.
He has mercy on those who fear him
in every generation.
He has shown the strength of his arm,
he has scattered the proud in their conceit.
He has cast down the mighty from their thrones,
and has lifted up the lowly.
He has filled the hungry with good things,
and the rich he has sent away empty.
He has come to the help of his servant Israel
for he has remembered his promise of mercy,
the promise he made to our fathers,
to Abraham and his children for ever.

The title of this prayer—Magnificat—is the Latin word for "proclaim." It is derived from Mary's response to Elizabeth's greeting during the visitation. The Church sings Mary's song during Evening Prayer, also known as Vespers.